THE POET'S VIEW

Also by GLADYS MARY COLES

POETRY

The Sounding Circle
Sinerva And Other Poems
The Snow Bird Sequence
Stoat, in Winter —
Liverpool Folio
Studies in Stone
Leafburners: New and Selected Poems
The Glass Island

BIOGRAPHY AND CRITICISM

The Flower of Light: A Biography of Mary Webb
Introductions to Mary Webb's novels *Gone to Earth*
        and *Precious Bane*
Introduction to Mary Webb's essays *The Spring of Joy*
Mary Webb: a new biography
Walks with Writers (with Gordon Dickins)
Mary Webb and Her Shropshire World

AS EDITOR

Both Sides of the River: Merseyside in Poetry & Prose
Poet's England: Lancashire
Wirral: An Anthology
Mary Webb: Collected Prose and Poems
Selected Poems of Mary Webb

THE POET'S VIEW

*Poems for Paintings
in the Walker Art Gallery, Liverpool*

Compiled & Edited
by
GLADYS MARY COLES

HEADLAND

First published in 1996 by
Headland Publications,
38 York Avenue, West Kirby,
Wirral, Merseyside, L48 3JF.

British Library Cataloguing in Publication Data.
A full CIP record for this book is available from the British Library.

ISBN: 0 903074 85 0

HEADLAND acknowledges the financial
assistance of North West Arts Board

Cover illustration: detail from *Isabella* by John Everett Millais.

Printed in Great Britain by
L. Cocker & Co., Berry Street, Liverpool.

The Walker Art Gallery

FOREWORD

I am delighted that it has been possible to publish this anthology of poems linked to Walker Art Gallery pictures. Gladys Mary Coles has done an excellent job. She has brought a major project to fruition here, as the anthology contains poems written at her invitation by nationally established poets; poems by those who took part in a series of workshops she tutored at the Gallery (poets from many areas of Britain, as well as the USA, attended); and also poems by young poets from Sefton High Schools. Long may she succeed in her endeavours to unite the sister arts.

FRANK MILNER
Senior Education Officer,
National Museums and Galleries on Merseyside

INTRODUCTION

The Walker Art Gallery, a fine neo-classical building, faces the St George's Hall and Plateau, among other Victorian buildings of architectural magnificence in the centre of Liverpool.

The Gallery took three years to build and was the gift of Alderman Andrew Barclay Walker. It was officially opened by the Earl of Derby on 6 September 1877, to great rejoicing. Immense crowds gathered for the opening ceremony, there were day-long celebrations, and poems to mark the occasion, written by local people, were published in the newspapers. This enthusiasm was indicative of the strong cultural and artistic life of Liverpool, a continuing tradition.

Today the Walker Art Gallery forms part of the National Museums and Galleries on Merseyside, its national status a recognition of the importance and high quality of its collections. These represent the finest in Western European art, comprising many different schools and periods, from the Middle Ages and Renaissance up to the present. The elegant rooms and their displays include a recently refurbished Sculpture Gallery.

'The Walker' is particularly rich in Victorian art, in which the narrative element is strong, drawn from Biblical, Classical and mythological sources, social themes, historical events, and literature. Especially splendid and comprehensive is the collection of Pre-Raphaelite works, Liverpool having fostered the movement from its beginning (when London critics rejected it). Liverpool Academy artists formed their own Pre-Raphaelite School, the only one in the provinces. Notable, too, are the Impressionist, Post-Impressionist and Symbolist works. Numerous important twentieth century artists are represented, with examples of the best in contemporary British art, acquired by purchase prizes in the biennial John Moores Liverpool Exhibitions from 1957 onwards, (two of the winning pictures are reproduced here).

To step through the Walker is to traverse the centuries, encountering outstanding pictures such as 'And when did you last see your father?', 'Faithful unto Death', 'Dante and Beatrice', 'Napoleon crossing the Alps', 'The Triumph of the Innocents'. I know that I speak for many others in stating that the Walker was immensely significant in my early development - Sunday afternoons and school holidays were wonderfully illumined by visits to the Gallery, an enriching and deeply formative experience.

I have always been interested, as a poet, in the correspondences between poetry and painting, the parallel artistic concerns and processes, both arts being rooted in observation, feeling, selection of image and detail. It was a natural progression when, tutoring a poetry writing course for the University of Liverpool, I decided to take a closer look, through poet's eyes, at the Walker collections, and so brought the workshop to the Gallery. Out of this successful experimental session grew the project 'Poems for Paintings', in which I tutored a series of workshops at the Gallery, exploring the relationship between poetry and works of art. These were open to the public and were arranged by Frank Milner and the Education Service

(NMGM). The workshops were all fully booked, participant poets coming not only from Merseyside but across the North West, from other parts of Britain, and the U.S.A.

In these sessions I discussed a variety of approaches and ways of interpreting the pictures in poetry (an enormously capacious art), and the appropriate forms, such as narratives, monologues, lyrics, poems in personal, reflective and interrogative voices, dialogues with the artist, the figures in the paintings, the sitters. I urged the poets not merely to describe but, in drawing verbal images from visual ones, to be 'truly inhabiting the painting' (as Dannie and Joan Abse recommend in *Voices in the Gallery,* 1986). The experience was one of close engagement and observation, sometimes involving research.

Subsequently I worked with the poets on their poems, shaping successive drafts. The workshops were followed by a memorable closing session of discussion and reading of the poems, after which I made a selection of the pieces for publication.

I then invited some nationally known poets to write poems for the anthology. These poets responded marvellously to the challenge, as I sent each of them a set of postcards of selected paintings in the Walker, from which to choose, and promptly the commissioned poems arrived. Special thanks, then, to Wendy Cope, U.A. Fanthorpe, Simon Rae, Dannie Abse, Carole Satyamurti, Roger Elkin, Lachlan Mackinnon and Nicholas Murray. My next step was to invite several well-known North West poets to take up the challenge, and again some very effective poems resulted.

The anthology contains sixty poems written in direct response to Walker paintings, plus three poems from published work, which I gathered because I think they make strong connections with specific pictures. For instance, whenever I look at 'Woman Ironing' by Degas I am reminded of a fine poem by Seamus Heaney, 'Old Smoothing Iron'. I felt privileged to be given permission to include this poem which so perfectly counterpoints U.A. Fanthorpe's commissioned work on the Degas picture.

Widening the scope of the anthology, I decided to include poems by young people written during a 'Poetry and Art' project (a collaboration between the Youth and the Advisory Services of Sefton, and the Education Service at the Walker). This involved the poet-painter Adrian Henri and three Sefton Secondary Schools. The poems were written by pupils from the Ambrose Barlow High School (Netherton) and Manor High School (Crosby), year 9, age 14, and Range High School, (Formby), year 12, age 17. The inspired idea for this schools' project was that of Joyce Smith, then Advisory teacher for English, and it came about with the help of Simon Kensdale, Youth Service Arts Fieldworker, Paul Higgins, Adviser for English, and teachers Anne Webb, Eddie Bannister and Jenny Jones. I enjoyed reading the poems and making my selection for this anthology.

I have arranged the anthology chronologically, with poems and reproductions of the paintings in juxtaposition. Sometimes there are two, or even three poems for one painting, showing a variety of individual vision and expression; testimony, too, of the picture's power.

It is my hope that readers will find the poets' responses to these works of art both illuminating and stimulating to the imagination; and that through these new dimensions we will return to the originals with deepened enjoyment and appreciation.

GLADYS MARY COLES

I wish to express my thanks for the encouragement and help of various kinds I received from the Staff of the Walker Art Gallery and National Museums and Galleries on Merseyside, and in particular from Frank Milner (Senior Education Officer), Peter Betts (Education Officer). Janet Bennett (Assistant Curator), Barbara Webb and Sam Line. For their kind assistance, I am grateful to Bridget Riley and Dave Lyon, Dannie Abse, Pat Adams, Simon Rae, Colin Wilkinson, Richard Lloyd-Jones, Adrian Henri, and Angela Heslop (BBC Radio Merseyside).

My thanks also to Joyce Smith,(not least for her poem 'Echo and Narcissus'), to the young poets for permission to include their pieces, and to Adrian Henri who worked with them and who kindly allowed me to include his poem 'The Triumph of the Innocents'.

ACKNOWLEDGEMENTS

Grateful acknowledgement is made to the Board of Trustees of the National Museums and Galleries on Merseyside for permission to reproduce forty-two paintings in the Walker Art Gallery Collections.

For kind permission to reproduce paintings in which the copyright is held by the artist:

David Hockney for *'Peter getting out of Nick's Pool'*, 1966 (Acrylic, 84"x 84") © David Hockney

Bridget Riley for *Sea Cloud'*, 1981 (Oil on linen, 67 1/8"x 67 1/4") © Bridget Riley

To Seamus Heaney and Faber and Faber Ltd. for permission to include 'Old Smoothing Iron' from *Station Island* (1984)

To Dannie Abse and Hutchinson & Co Ltd for permission to include 'Watching a Woman Putting on Lipstick' from *Ask The Bloody Horse* (1986)

To Adrian Henri and Bloodaxe Books for 'The Triumph of the Innocents', first published in *Not Fade Away* (1994)

To Brian Wake and Headland Publications for 'Don't Look, Jump', first published in *Into Hiding* (1992)

Gladys Mary Coles' poem 'One Summer Day' was a prizewinner in the Lancaster Literature Festival Competition 1995 and first appeared in the anthology *Poems 18 (Lancaster Litfest 1995).*

CONTENTS

PITY

The waiting is over,
Mother and Son at last released
From the long agony of the Cross.

Mary's cloak, as heavy as her grief,
Spreads like a great black stain
Upon the conscience of the world.

Across her knee, in all the humility of death,
The pale pierced body of Jesus lies.
His open eyes see nothing — and see everything.

Against all hope she looks for some
Small flutter in that quiet breast,
Holds his wrist to feel a pulse, however faint.

His lifeless hand has dropped, to touch
The white hem of his Mother's dress,
As if in reverence and love.

The pity is that it should end like this —
The story that began in that small stable,
Warm with the breath of animals,
Bright with the sumptuous cloth of Kings.

No Kings are here in this stark landscape,
Only three faint crosses
Lingering like an aching dream
Against the indifferent sky.

Bessie Hall

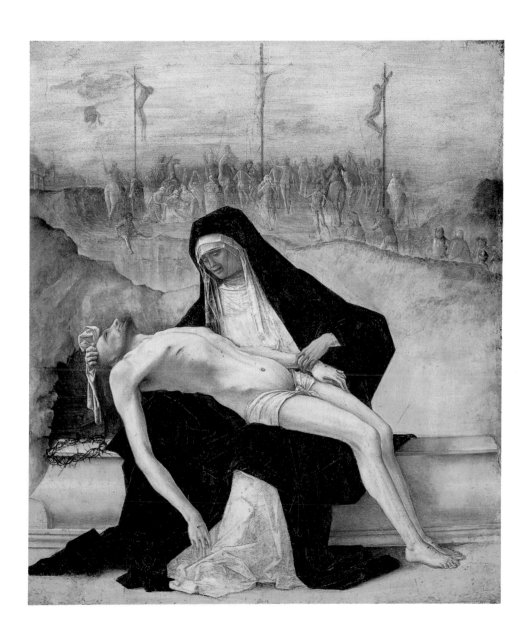

Portrait of a Young Man, (c 1520), Jan Mostaert, (c. 1473-1555/6)
(detail)

PORTRAIT OF A YOUNG MAN

Classic features.
Composed countenance.
Impeccably correct demeanour.
A young nobleman at prayer.

Garments of finest velvet, costly satin
in unflamboyant style.
A jewelled ring half-hidden
by a muslin glove.
His *Prie Dieu* a dry stone wall.

An elaborate scenario behind his equanimity.
A scene of self-indulgent revelry.
A hunting party picnic in a forest clearing.
Alongside, the legend of Saint Hubert,
a nobleman converted by a vision
to a life of self-denying piety.

Enigmatic contradictions.
Ambivalence and indecision.
The young man's mind
is torn apart by twin desires.
What might have been
his future (now long past)
remains unwritten history.

Mary Richardson Brown

HENRY VIII

The Painter thinks...
The King, proud, arrogant, boastful
The King, fists clenched, clamped shut
The King, shoulders straight and chest out
The King, expensive clothes, jewels, five rings
The King stares directly at me with small beady eyes
I know this painting must be good.

The Mistress thinks...
My love, so proud, three hours now he's stood unmoving.
My love's wife stands next to me but still
My love's eyes have never left me
He makes me feel vibrant and passionate.

The Queen thinks...
My husband has stood for three hours unmoving
My husband stares but not at me
My husband's four previous wives have all fared badly
My husband's fifth wife may end the same.
I must bear a boy.

Lawrence Evans
(St. Ambrose Barlow High School)

HENRY VIII

There stands his great fatness
Trying to look impressive in his finest
Jewelled clothing.
With padding to make his shoulders broader,
Rope to make his waist thinner.
A codpiece to show manhood,
A dagger to look masterful,
A clenched fist to look stronger.
There stands his illusion.

Joanne Morrison
(St. Ambrose Barlow High School)

THE MAGDALEN

Well, I've done it!
Spent every last farthing.
I've never held anything so precious.
I'm terrified I'll drop it.
See Thomas frown at me —
He suspects I've stolen it, no doubt.

It seemed like a wonderful idea at the time.
But how will they see it?
Call me a silly show-off?
Judas will complain about the cost.
They don't think much of me.
But He ...

Well, they don't show Him
Much appreciation;
Falling out among themselves,
Wanting to be top of the table.
Someone has to show him,
Like Samuel anointed David.

He poured love over me.
He didn't look askance
As if I'd crawled out
From under the carpet.
What does it matter
What they think!

Mary Brett

Self-portrait as a young man, (c. 1630), Rembrandt van Rijn (1606-69)
(detail)

ON A RECENT VIEWING OF
'SELF PORTRAIT 1630' BY REMBRANDT

The hair unruly and the eyes reserved
Framed high above the master, you were raised
Like a shy icon for the Lower Fifth:
Focus of every bored, bewildered gaze.

Last time I scanned your face I was in search
Of a lost subjunctive: the day before
You'd proved unwilling to provide the dates
Of the second Carthaginian War.

Disappointingly inarticulate!
But as an adolescent I could warm
To you, and your great conk, but most of all
To that nervous sense of an impending storm.

When the big bombs came and the soft ground shook
Back to class from assembly in the hall
We braced ourselves to face another day:
Made certain you sat straight upon the wall.

Alan Davis

LANDSCAPE WITH THE ASHES OF PHOCION

Phocion, the deposed Athenian leader, was forced to drink hemlock. He was further disgraced by the refusal of a public burial. His body was taken to Megara and unceremoniously burnt. Poussin's picture shows his widow recovering the ashes. In one version of the story she eats them.

1. The sun's procrastinations through the sky
   mock my few appointed widow's tasks.

   I marvel at the time time takes to pass.
   Each hour's a rock,

   an olive press,
   and what comes out

   is the pure essence of grief.
   I hover on the threshold of two rooms

   uncertain which contains the least
   amount of pain, Forgetting

   is the worst;
   it means remembering again.

   Meat festers on my fork...

   I wonder, when the Titan's eagle came
   did it keep to an appointed hour?

   And were his nights of healing
   undisturbed? My eagle swoops

   without warning, tearing and tugging,
   and my nights heal nothing.

2. The condemning mouths
   were tight with envy,

   little openings
   pipetting spite

   behind arms raised
   in loyal salutes.

   He drank the hemlock
   that I couldn't share.

   Not one of them
   could meet his eye.

3. Cur-beaten down to this:
   a starving creature circling a fire
   weighing the danger
   against the drag of hunger.

   My maid's so jumpy I could slap her.
   Stop whimpering, I hiss
   before I realize
   it's me. Come *on.*

4. So here we are.

   They brought him to this place
   between the trees
   and burnt him like refuse.

   I kneel in reverence in the cinder-bed
   and drive my fingers down in search
   of some last lingering warmth.

   My tears have formed a paste
   which I shall eat and relish
   as I did my marriage feast:

ground pumice on my tongue,
grit scratting between my teeth,
throat scoured with the bitter salts —

a madwoman in her final throes...

No doubt the spy who's lurking
at a coward's distance
will depict my ash-pit antics,
my clown's tipped nose
and smudged heroic beard,
in such a way
as to amuse his masters.

My maid's aghast,
her face a mirror
of the horror of my own.

Hands on each other's shoulders,
our arms form the trembling rim
of a bowl set soundlessly ringing
to the pitch of destruction.

Our mouths fall open and I feel
the silence splintering, but cannot tell
into what retched noise, whether
owl-whoop, wolf-howl, womb-wail,
or shriek of appalling laughter
to detonate the smoke-blackened
rafters of rooks...

Simon Rae

David Garrick as Richard III, (1745), William Hogarth (1697-1764)
(detail)

GARRICK'S RICHARD

'For Dickon, thy master, is bought and sold'
              — Shakespeare, *Richard III*

This actor's eloquent eyes, gentle features
are closer to the real Richard Neville
than Shakespeare's depiction of a villain.

No crouchback either, but straight and soldierly
(as witnessed by many). Political caricature,
Tudor concoction, perpetuated in poetry
in a play to please a Queen. Those deaths —
assassinations? The young princes, his nephews
sickening in the Tower. The blame on his shoulders.

No snake in the grass, though serpentine,
stretched out by Hogarth in a sinuous line,
the artist seeing beauty in this shape
and in his friend, the convincing actor
who here is surely pleading Richard's innocence?

Gladys Mary Coles

Molly Long Legs, (c. 1760-62), George Stubbs (1724-1806)
(detail)

MOLLY LONG LEGS

he's holding my bit too tight
so my lips are clamped in this false grin
that's why my eyes are rolling white
although I must admit
the chief cause of my embarrassment
is my tail -
stumped by the stable scissors
according to the fashion (don't the rich
appreciate the aesthetic balance of nature?)
similarly my mane is combed flat
like a barber's parting

if I could speak, Mr Stubbs, I would request
you paint my old tail back
and dance my tawny locks in the wind

Dymphna Callery

The Lincolnshire Ox, (c. 1790), George Stubbs (1724-1806)

THE LINCOLNSHIRE OX

His Lincoln Ox is hanging on the wall;
my portrait's been down-graded to the hall.
He is besotted with the beast he'd won
on bets at cockfighting - it weighs a ton.
This living mountain dwarfs the lake and park,
prize cockerel a dot, husband a thumbmark.

Eight horses carted it to London town.
My Lord felt deprived, ever wore a frown
although paid well; now Royal Ox, stabled
by a Duke; he made me view the fabled
beast again, exhibited for all to fawn,
admire its size, brute strength and span of horn.

And when the animal was slain, he grieved,
would not eat meat for days - appeared bereaved
as of dear friend; he dressed himself in black
until revived by advent of a sack,
four hooves and horns inside, so pleased, buffoon,
you'd think he had been left a big fortune.

My portrait's back now in its rightful place;
Shrine of Ox takes up some library space.

Fay Eagle

RUINS (HOLYROOD CHAPEL)

Ruins
whether of stone
or ageing bone, have grandeur
a dark grace of endurance.

        This historic chapel
framed in dour wood, stands
sombre on a plane of subdued colour.
    Stone-cold chancel
     small primeval altar
lit by a lamp of ivory oil;
long aisles of glimmering matins.
Lady Chapel, sacrosanct — cloisterless
staring wide, yet still a chapel royal
bare of jewel glass
and flitting acolyte.

Yet, surely there is ...
gothic horror here
ancient fear and modern awe
of perpendicular hollows ... doorless
roofless ... eyries of a higher hawk, endless
heartless phantoms. Crude pigment
grotto of dry harebells, coif
of lichen-snail and granite nettle.
Overall — death's brush
too early and too long
another mourningsong
for loveliness — not yet risen.

A ruined chapter house
    of gospel truth
    open to the sky
where a Queen once walked
and hoped for Paradise.

Gina Riley

DINING WITH THE ENEMY

How will we do it, topple this schemer?
He's having his *last* meal at our table.
Our young sister's caught by this sly charmer —
courting her will bring him more than trouble,
Lorenzo, mere apprentice to our trade;
fool Isabella, so beguiled, in love.
Their love? see my falcon tearing a dove —
with my brother I'll rip him from her side.

She knows the family needs her to wed high —
a noble of Siena, bringing wealth,
securing our future, should trade run dry.
Oh, Isabella, loyalty's not felt.
You've forced us to devise a deadly plan —
Emilio broods on it as he sips wine.

Each in the other is so closely bound
(she hangs upon his wily whisperings)
neither notices that I kick her hound.
Lorenzo gives her sliced blood oranges —
emblem of his fate. None can halt its course.
Near the Arno's bank, north of Firenze,
in thick forest we'll chop him from his horse.
This will please our uncle Corleone.

Gladys Mary Coles

NAPOLEON CROSSING THE ALPS

Wordsworth crossed the Alps in seventeen ninety,
Ardent and young and enthusiastic
New dedicate to truth and poetry.
Napoleon poised for conquest, frantic
For glory, riding a donkey but not
Like Christ eschewing military might,
His mind on bloody wars and peace forgot;
The fearsome Alps with snow bedecked and bright,
No barrier to his thrusting ambition;
The peasant and the ass obey his word.
He leads his army in the direction
Of Italy to victory by the sword.

The force of thought outlasts the warrior's power,
The poet triumphs from his lonely tower.

Geraldine Wilby

The Stonebreaker, (1857-58), John Brett (1831-1902)

THE STONEBREAKER

Dear Inchbold,
                    I want you to know about this.

23 miles from London I was walking
with Black Spot when I lingered to gaze at
a steep scarp of the chalky Downs.
I gazed and gazed until I seemed tò stand
                    . just outside Eden.

Faraway, the beech trees in their summer
magnificence while, nearby, there happened to be
a pile of stones and a barely living tree.
It sprang out of a dead one.

                    Oh Inchbold,
do you believe in the Resurrection?

Remember mild Tom, the model who died,
the one who resembled my young brother?
Suddenly, from nowhere, he appeared
and, with a noiseless hammer, struck the stones.
He did not look pathetic like the Stonebreaker
portrayed by Henry Wallis but wore fake,
unsoiled, peasant's clothes.

                    Before I could speak
a bullfinch alighted on a high branch
of the strange, frail tree and Tom vanished.

You doubt what I saw?   I doubt what I saw.
So much is mirage and shadow.   The law
of gravity asserts itself in my mind.
I know the far hills are not really blue,
that sunlight does not truly paint the grass
an indistinct yellow.   Love, itself, errs.
A child's swift daubs on paper are not Art
though the mother may think so.

                    Oh Inchbold,
did I see what I saw?   Tom breaking stones?

          I beg you, tell no-one of this.   You know
how some believe we artists are crazy!
Besides, I may paint this experience though
Ruskin says mine is mirror's work not man's.
Write me soon. Your loving friend,

                    John Brett.

                              Dannie Abse

Sweethearts and Wives, (1860), John Lee (active 1850-70)

SWEETHEARTS AND WIVES

You are my sweetheart and my wife
And I cherish you so
Give me a kiss my lovely for I
really don't want to go.

The sea, the sea is calling,
And the ship stands way out there.
Give me a kiss my lovely,
To let me know you care.

Can we bear this parting?
Will our love stand the strain?
Give me a kiss my lovely
Don't let us feel the pain.

Months I'll be away my lovely,
Will you to me be true?
Give me a kiss my lovely,
Tell me it's the same for you.

Clare Owens

Corner of a Cornfield, (c. 1860), William Davis (1812-73)

CORNER OF A CORNFIELD

To sit and touch
        a moment of tranquillity,
        a quiet corner, part of a wider plan.
        Drowsing air, heavy with peace
        and wave upon wave
        of blades of maize
        washing the canvas, fresh
        in cool clear green.

To step inside
        the frame and lie outstretched
        and suck a straw and dream
        of buttered cobs and bowls of flakes
        awash with cream, and hear
        the rustle of a harvest mouse
        and watch a waterfall
        of tumbling sunlight gleam.

And wish away
        the day when darkening shadows
        scar the meadows, when progress
        wipes the canvas clean
        and tarmaced roads
        reach for the sun, and seeds
        sleep deep in concrete beds,
        and no lark rises singing.

Jean Stanbury

Faithful unto Death, (1865), Edward J. Poynter (1836-1919)

ONE SUMMER DAY

I remember the time exactly.
We were just finishing a meal,
nectarines and grapes in our hands,
white wine in sparkling goblets.
We were sitting in the garden of Julia Felix
under the shade of her new verandah —
she, with pride, showing us her gold snake ring,
the presents brought back by her husband
from Greece. Another ring, a cameo of her profile,
her tresses exquisite in sardonyx. As she held it up,
the filigreed gold and creamy stone against a sky
as blue as lapis lazuli, we stared
fixed by her white hand, the gleaming ring
and a dark fungus of cloud behind,
growing rapidly, its core of flame spurting.

The ground shook, our goblets scattered —
we were running in panic, rocks raining down.
Constantly the cloud threw out its destruction
like a God vengeful against our summer world,
the sumptuous sinning. Choking, we escaped,
taking boats south to Amalfi, where we heard
today of the ash burying Pompeii.

Our cousin Marcello was on sentry duty — we saw him
as we fled; called to him, but he didn't hear us,
standing against the orange glare. At his post.
What a privilege to die that way!
But, sad to say, we lost our faithful Paurus
chained, guarding the door of our villa.
We will come to Roma, dear Father,
be assured. We send our love to Nerina.
Your son, Petronius, at Positano.

Gladys Mary Coles

A VIEW OF THE PRE-RAPHAELITES

Canvases, larger than life,
and their themes:
gorgeous, extraordinary,
detailing every aspect
and facet of the heart,
agonised and glorified:
legend, myth and storybook.

Maidens and their suitors,
extravagant, enigmatic
and beautiful,
brim with love's explosion,
wither with its expulsion,
love's ceaseless delight, endless anguish.
Despair
of unrewarded loyalty,
or poison bite of jealousy,
traitor stab of
betrayal's double blade.

You, my more than sister
hear none of his frantic whispers:
consumed by passion's fire
and desire
for me, and mine for him.

Carole Baldock

THE TRIUMPH OF THE INNOCENTS

'The Triumph of the Innocents':
how weary that inner sense
of triumph, despite the leering faces
amongst the crowd, the whispered voices
in the night, the fight to paint
each chubby thigh, each rainbow bubble,
to get it right, despite the siren songs,
the alien smells, the endless trouble.
Why did the canvas split just there?
Sometimes I feel not even my best friends
care, cannot see my plight. To make
each infant real and yet ethereal
as moonlight. Even more difficult
to fight this lonely fight with him;
Jacob's with the Angel no worse than mine.

Once more to the mastic and the turpentine...

Adrian Henri

THE TRIUMPH OF THE INNOCENTS

Prosaic parents plod the dusty road to Egypt:
Caught in the mortal web of a threatening present
They travel, unwilling, to an unknown future.
Not blessed, as their infant son, with assurance,
They cannot float on the sea of eternity,
Nor can they know the bubble-blowing bliss
Of the ever-young, nor see
The joy in the baby's face.
He is enchanted by his fellow-travellers
Playing in the waters of the everlasting now.

Mary Brett

And When Did You Last See Your Father?, (1878),
William Frederick Yeames (1835-1918)

'AND WHEN DID YOU LAST SEE YOUR FATHER?'

I've posed the question, boy! Make haste, reply!
The footstool's there, now we are eye to eye.
Intimidation's furthest from my mind.
With hat and gloves removed, I'm being kind.

Your family's foes around your table sit,
Hoping that you'll disclose, by trick or wit
Of mine, your father's whereabouts and more,
So hastening the end to Civil War.

At the door your anxious kinsfolk stand.
Your mother, calmly with a gentle hand,
Restrains your elder sister, hides her grief.
Your little sister has begun to weep.

The soldier, tool and executioner of power,
Mere guardian of small children at this hour,
Does as he's bid, no more, no less;
With blind obedience, he'll cause distress, if necessary.

Now Thomas here, has searched the house in vain.
Quick ways to make you speak, to me made plain.
Slumped, sprawled — frustrated cruelty,
His foe denied his hopes for victory.

I search your face, which innocence portrays;
You trust in me, doubt not my honest ways.
Your soul shines through but more than this. I stare:
A likeness to my own young son, you bear.

What smites me through, your pure, young, guileless eyes
Can see my face but cannot realize,
I tempt you to betray or otherwise tell lies.

I grasp, at last, the great enormity
Of using one as innocent as thee,
To catch and hold and kill my enemy.

This most unsavoury quest must cease.
Pray, Royalist child, I bid you, hold your peace!
Your answer — silence be!

Antoinette Loftus

'AND WHEN DID YOU LAST SEE YOUR FATHER?'

I am a soldier of the King
and Father said
I must never be afraid
though Cromwell's Men
are present in control.

The demands of *When?* and
Where? are sword thrusts
to chill the blood.

Be still my beating heart
in answer to their wiles
and let me tell the truth
as close as I dare today.

Please God protect my Father
and his son
and not give those I love
away.

Margaret Ross

Eventide: a Scene in the Westminster Union, (1878),
Sir H. Van Herkomer (1849-1914)   (detail)

EVENTIDE: AN INTERPRETATION

Molly, Annie, Sarah Jane,
try to reach their daily sewing goals,
in spite of pain from threading needles
with arthritic hands.
Old eyes are dimmed with strain
from lifetimes spent in plying seamstress trade
in dark and dripping sweatshop holes.

Daisy cuts the cloth, a dear young orphan maid,
organizing fuddled brains to deal with daily jobs,
promising their bowls of porridge will be sweet;
toothless gums need pobby food.
On Sunday there'll be buttered bread,
instead of watery grog,
perhaps some milk, a little meat,
depending on the Master's mood.

Her daily Bible passage read,
Alice sits and dreams, as ghosts, like lantern slides,
process across her memories' screen.

Four young children disturb her eventide,
like steps of stairs, within a decade's span,
taken by fever, one frightful year, all dead.
They kneel in line to say their prayers,
kiss their Papa, then off to bed.
Their smiles shine out across the years
as William, her eldest boy, appears
resplendent in his uniform, with loaded knapsack;
he waves, just as he did when off to fight
the Ruskie war... did not come back.

Alice sees her husband, John.
His face is always on her mind.
Though he's alive, he might as well have died
as live in that depressing place, reserved for men.
Just once a week, they meet in church and find
that when the time to part arrives,
the wound is opened once again.
She prays that soon the time will come
when they can meet forever on the other side.

Old Betsy has a birthday, she's been told.
Her Sunday bonnet makes it plain
there's something special on.
A nephew calls and brings some flowers.
He buys a pot of tea, rare as gold,
for her and best friend Sarah Jane.
He used to be her favourite;
now she tries to place his face,
etched on the shifting sands of memory,
and wonders why she's in this place.

She sips her dish of tea and suddenly recalls
that from m'lady's belt, in service days
there hung a caddy key...
        ...and then the curtain falls.

Albert Morgan

Dante and Beatrice, (1884), Henry Holiday (1839-1927)
(detail)

DANTE AND BEATRICE

Seven times the circling of the century
Since Dante stood in classic pose to stare,
Captured by strokes of romantic artistry,
As Beatrice passed in Florence, unaware
The inspirational seed sown in his heart,
For one day his spiritual love he would declare.

Her bold companion tossed her head erotically
While she who followed gazed in blue despair.
Gemma, his bride? Unsung in his poetry.
Man's iconic worship's hard to bear.
Beatrice, his guide through Hell and Purgatory
And Paradise and all of history.

Mary White

DANTE AND BEATRICE

Ay up! I think he fancies yo
      the maid in waiting's heard to say,
      while Beatie, speeding on her way,
replies: *He knows where he can go.*

The silly B, does she not know
      that yon poor chap she spurns, one day,
      may from the straight and narrow stray,
if she gives him the old heave-ho?

He burns with love and longs to tell,
but, when it comes to pulling birds,
      alas, he hasn't got the knack.
It's awful being lost for words.
And yet, for her he'd go to Hell,
      and write a poem on t' way back.

Graham Casey

Samson, (c. 1886-87), Solomon J. Solomon (1860-1927)
(detail)

SAMSON

The queue's motley, that slowly serpentines
Past Samson, bound and shorn, straining to free
Himself from five, flexed, grasping Philistines
Stops at the canvas. Everyone must see
The painting, pass a judgement and be judged.
A soldier, the buxom local girls,
A newly married man — none will have budged
Till the Jew's predicament (which unfurls
Continually before his eyes and theirs)
Has been interpreted. The villains swarm;
The victim, overwhelmed, tires and despairs.
Delilah waves a wild triumphant arm
Her real emotions bare now as her breasts
Thrust jeering at the lover she detests.

Alan Davis

SAMSON AND DELILAH

What have you done my love
Oblivious to all around
Samson wounded by his love of Delilah
Her sadistic pleasure apparent
In a scene of chaos

His locks of power lay shorn
Held up to ridicule by his mistress
The smell of perfume sweet in their bed
Turns sour with the sweat of struggle
In a scene of disarray

The aftermath to betrayal
Lay in the Temple
One day chained and forgotten
Samson took his revenge
In a scene of retribution

Peter J. Hewitt, (U.S.A.)

Fantine, (1886), Margaret Bernadine Hall (1863-1910)
(detail)

HUGO'S FANTINE

She still is beautiful;
she loved but once, and he
deserted her, endowed her with
a bastard girl.
The painter lights her head,
her blonde hair gleams in wisps
beneath her cap; but she is wearing
black, the remnants of the fripperies
of fashion cut down to clothe her babe.
One roughened hand protects the crib;
her deep blue eyes are blurred with
unshed tears; Cosette, bonnetted,
long-lashed, sleeps in the trust of
innocence, her chubby hands outstretched
on soft pink coverlet; a red-cheeked
doll discarded on the floor.

Darkness surrounds them.
The eyes of Fantine haunt;
she knows she must give up her child;
the shame of being unmarried outcasts her.
She does not yet know, to pay
for Cosette's care she'll sell her dowry
of golden hair and two of her front teeth
of pearl, for love.

Fay Eagle

FANTINE

Gentle guardian of this sleeping child
How many eyes have you beguiled?

Crowned with halo of mellow light
On once fair hair no longer bright.

Those eyes so tired, so sad, so real,
The misery of your plight reveal.

So many stories I have formed
Around your beauty so forlorn

Of how you watch over the ailing babe,
Praying for the Lord to save

This your only infant child,
So pallid, as her fever rises.

Or are you left a starving mother
By careless, cruel, abandoning lover?

Ann Davies

COSETTE, DAUGHTER OF FANTINE

Offspring of my wayward wanderings,
Begotten of my illicit activities,
So tender and beautiful are you,
Soft as gossamer fairy's web,
Gentle and lovely and I gaze
In wonder at your perfect form.

My body buys your fine clothes
My love for you my child is true,
Content am I to sell myself daily
To give you what I consider you need.

Beauty, do I possess it? not like yours my little one.
Some tell me "Yes" so eagerly
While others quickly use the commodity I sell
Then hurriedly depart to follow their own stars.

My sun moon and stars are you,
Your delicate little fingers entwine around my heart
That sweet smile and your eyes aglow
When I return to you, give me joy.

While I am away do you miss me?
You are so treasured and perfect,
The delight of babyhood to me... and
I ponder daily at the miracle you are.

Thankful that in this squalid city of Paris
I have your sweetness to make my life worthwhile.
And the realisation dawns upon me,
Great God! my life is not inconsequential now.

Clare Owens

VENUS AND ANCHISES

Born to beauty on the ocean's foam, Venus
goddess of peace and love, floats in fragrance
through the forest. Silken robes swirl;
frilled hems like sea-shells dance
in a froth of gold.

At her feet flowers bloom into summer.
Pale apple blossoms spring from gnarled boughs,
the dry cold leaves of winter wither
and the waning moon
gives way to day.

Doves frame her way, lions pad
pregnant with power, all nature
bows to her sway and deep in shade
Anchises pays homage, spellbound,
like the fragile earth.

Golden encounter – goddess and mortal man
meet once again through the painter's art.
Divine union, Virgil's epic theme reveals
their glorious destiny — their ancestry
of the Roman race.

Love, the creative force, and Virgil tells
of Aeneas, their Trojan son,
who rescued his father from the flames of Troy;
who fought in Italy, until proud tribes
fell to his might.

Who braved the underworld, like Orpheus,
and crossed the Styx, the river of the dead,
to meet once more Anchises who
showed him a multitude of souls, the dead,
awaiting their re-birth.

Their progeny, pre-destined for fame,
Romulus and Remus, saved by a wolf.
Great Brutus; then a line
to the mighty Caesars,
and the golden age of Rome.

Painting of light and shade, bright
with promise for the Roman race, dark
the future for Anchises, blinded
for his proud boast
of union with the Gods.

Fabric of mighty Rome, stranded
with violent threads, the peace and conflict,
the discord, of a master race.

Jean Stanbury

Woman Ironing, (c. 1890), Edgar Degas (1832-1917)
(detail)

OLD SMOOTHING IRON

Often I watched her lift it
from where its compact wedge
rode the back of the stove
like a tug at anchor.

To test its heat she'd stare
and spit in its iron face
or hold it up next her cheek
to divine its stored danger.

Soft thumps on the ironing board.
Her dimpled angled elbow
and intent stoop
as she aimed the smoothing iron

like a plane into linen,
like the resentment of women.
To work, her dumb lunge says,
is to move a certain mass

through a certain distance,
is to pull your weight and feel
exact and equal to it.
Feel dragged upon. And buoyant.

Seamus Heaney
(from *Station Island*, 1984)

Woman Ironing, (c. 1890), Edgar Degas (1832-1917)

WOMAN IRONING

I thought I knew what was coming when he said
He wanted to do my likeness at the ironing.
I live in the city, people tell you things. Me looking at him,
It would be, across the ironing board, my hair and my eyes
In a good light, and something a bit off the shoulder.

But it wasn't. He rushed around drawing curtains.
Made it hard to iron. O yes, I had to keep ironing.
He needed to see the strength, he said. Kept on
About my dynamic right shoulder, then left it out,
Though you can see where he ought to have put it.

Come on, what's-your-name, he kept saying,
Show us that muscle-power! That's what I'm after.
I might've been an engine, not a person.
No, I didn't take to him. I'm used to rudeness,
But he was making such a sketch of me.

If someone's paying you, it isn't easy
To speak your mind. Still, *Sir,* I said,
*I really don't want to see my hair like that,
All scraped back, like a hot person's hair,
And anyone can tell that under my arms I'm sweating.*

Hair? Sweat? That's how it is when you iron,
Says he. *You're not here to tell me what to do.
I'll make you permanent, the way you look
When you're ironing. O yes,* he says, *I'll show you
The way you look when no one's watching.*

                                        U. A. Fanthorpe

An Idyll, (1891), Maurice Grieffenhagen (1862-1931)

AN IDYLL

My finest yet — a title's all it lacks.
Have you noticed the echoing reds:
her hair in his taut grasp
the swollen sun,
poppies' gaily bleeding mouths?

And his muscles — silk, nothing brutish;
gold dints and angles framing
her half-naked breast,
pale centre the eye's drawn to.
Do you see the lambs? A touch of Eden.

'Ravished'? 'The Violation'? Fool!
Surely it's obvious in every line —
the sacrificial languor of her arms,
her trance-averted gaze, those lips,
the poppies' welcoming throats,
all saying yes... yes.

Carole Satyamurti

Punishment of Lust, (1891), Giovanni Segantini (1858-99)

EXPENSE OF SPIRIT

Only a stern and over-righteous brush
could have painted these high shores,
this drear place of abandon; only

a rigid palette depict the world's
blue-black rim as moral tundra where snow-
tides beach such flotsam-souls on clinker-grit

and shale: women's bodies chastened beyond
shame and shamelessness, in such pallid lineaments
of repose, corpses strewn on cold, brittle shingle

uncoiling shipwrecked locks of Medusa hair.

Matt Simpson

PUNISHMENT OF LUST

There is a clarity of light
An icy stillness in the air,
Beneath its snowy cloak the thorn
Holds fast the tendrils of their hair,
Twin figures, borne on unseen hands,
Drifting there, vanguard of the fair.
Oblivious of the cruel cold
As once they lay in luxury
Indifferent to another's pain.

What bitterness devised the theme
What slight impelled the painter's hand?
Half-clothed, in either death or dream,
They haunt this eerie frozen land.

Dora Kennedy

A Pageant of Childhood, (1899), Thomas Cooper Gotch (1854-1931)
(detail)

A CHILD'S JOURNEY

We move along, at first undaunted
full of wonder at the world
and all it has to offer.
We stand tall as we step out
across the marble stones of time.
Eager to announce our arrival.

The trumpets demand attention
and touch the lives around us
with a fanfare of hope
for the journey still ahead.
Our view of the world is bright
as we march towards tomorrow.

We proceed with caution
but still delight in the journey;
the cadence slows
our footsteps lighten.
We seek advice from others,
checking our pace against theirs.

Those who have travelled before us
provide the words to carry on.
We continue on the journey
a journey thrust upon us,
begun with the flush of youth
still burning in our hearts.

Cynthia D. Hewitt (U.S.A.)

Bathers, Dieppe, (1902), Walter R. Sickert (1860-1942)

LES VACANCES

Maman et Papa au bord de la mer.
Aujourd'hui il fait beau. I remember it well.
Voilà Armand, in the corner down there,
With Maman et Papa au bord de la mer!
Oh, *bored,* c'est le mot. I tear out the hair
As we limp through ce livre avec Mademoiselle.
Maman et Papa au bord de la mer.
Il fait beau. I remember it only too well.

Wendy Cope

NOT QUITE A SONNET, ON NOT QUITE A POSTCARD

Weather, as forecast, has been superb so far. In fact,
All week, we haven't seen a Corot cloud or Monet mist.
Loads of folk down here this weekend — natives I expect —
Though we picnicked *sur l'herbe* as usual. Almost
Every day the sky and sea have touched on aquamarines
Right down to the horizon. Some tasteful seafood
Restaurants: the turbot's good. And lobster, too. We
Swim most afternoons, though, even then, the sea
Is cold. Have gone *à la mode* and bought this season's
Costumes; stripes in blues and reds, but you'd barely
Know just yet that black is "out". The French brood
Enviously, stand parleying in groups. Since the *magazin's*
Run short of postcards, I'm sending you (not too late?)
This beach scene — think I've got the spume and shadows right —

Roger Elkin

WATERHOUSE

Beneath the water's face
he finds in these green depths
the soul refracts like light,
sees in his rippling eyes
the world within,
self upon bright self
breaking to his sight.
So the artist turns
from love to the lure
of water and illusion — the gaze
of painted creatures
meeting his own gaze.
The women he desires
he bathes in this same stream
that flows from canvas
to canvas, making of them
mermaids, sirens. They gleam
between tall reeds, milk-
white naiads playing
among the waterlilies,
dragonflies. Imploring pools
lap at their child's breasts.
Just once, as Hylas
he came to the brink
of caressing these pink-
nippled girls, the nymphs
he thirsted for. Yet as their
hands, cold as river pearls
reached to draw him
down, he knew
some colours move
only in water, are seen
only by those who drown.

Edmund Cusick

ECHO AND NARCISSUS

Echo waited on the bank for many years,
Holding dear Narcissus fast within her gaze,
Across the waters which divided them, and
        Hoped and longed for
        Him to love her.

Narcissus did not leave the study of his face,
'I have to know the kind of man I am', he said,
'Below, I see eyes full of love.'
        'Eyes full of love'
        Agreed his Echo.

'I must explore the secrets of my soul,
My hopes, my fears, my deep desires,
And know mine is the right philosophy.'
        'The right philosophy,'
        Agreed his Echo.

'I have to exercise the working of my mind,
Ponder problems to extend my thoughts,
Find answers and have fine ideas.'
        'Fine ideas,'
        Agreed his Echo.

She was content to sun him with her warmth,
To share his pleasures, feel his pain,
And hope that he might reach across the stream,
        Approve her, and
        Accept her care.

At last he looked at her and frowned,
'I know what you will say before you speak,
And you cast a shadow on this place. I'll find
        A clearer pool
        To be alone.'

In loss and grief she called upon the gods,
'How shall I live alone without my love?'
They told her, 'Echo, you have found your voice!
        Speak your own mind,
        Seek life and joy.'

Around, she saw the wonder of the world,
Heard music in the water and the trees,
Found the perfection, that Narcissus sought,
        In brief spring flowers,
        Then laughed, and sang
        Her own song.

Joyce Smith

REFLECTIONS: ECHO AND NARCISSUS:

I brought you here along with me
With this strange notion in my head
That if I couldn't make you hear me
I'd have to show it you instead

Echo and Narcissus
Lie trapped inside the frame
She couldn't make him hear her
And she couldn't shout his name

But even if she'd had a voice
Narcissus loved somebody else
He couldn't take his eyes off
The reflection of himself

The first time I saw that picture
their sad story rang so true
Echo and Narcissus
Are reflecting me and you

Perhaps it was naive to think
You would see what I am saying
You're more concerned
In why your button hole is fraying

I thought I saw you stare at them
Before we left that 'arty' place
But on closer inspection
You were just checking your face

I wish I had the ability
To turn you into a flower
Just getting you to notice me
Is way beyond my power

Helen Davenport
(Range High School)

ECHO AND NARCISSUS

As I gaze into the picture,
It just seems so unfair,
That Echo wasted all that love
On someone who didn't care.

I wake up from this dream,
I know what I must do,
I must stop something that's hopeless,
And free my thoughts from you.

Kate Smith
(Range High School)

Study of Two Sheep, (1911), Maxwell Gordon Lightfoot (1886-1911)

JUST SHEEP

Our portrait's finished now
we take our place
amongst the greats; the artist's
caught our enigmatic smile
our Mona Lisa look.

And Constable – he knew our drift,
that's us, the leaders of the flock.
Our cousin, twice removed,
did a great favour once – posed
for *The Scapegoat* – guided Holman Hunt.

So, fame assured
we safely graze on gallery walls.
Through half-closed eyes look down
to view the viewers pass, prick back our ears,
bask in their praise.

Jean Stanbury

Mrs Mounter, (1916-17), Harold Gilman (1876-1919)

MRS MOUNTER

Mrs Mounter comes twice a week.
When she leaves, there is a glossy shine
on furniture, black leaded grates
and a smell of carbolic soap.

"I'd like to paint your portrait Mrs Mounter."
"Paint me, Sir! In my kitchen? Are you sure?"
"Don't dress up. I want you as you are."

The easel fitted in behind the sink.
She sat behind the table laid for tea.
A large brown glazed pot.
Cups and saucers. A lustre jug.
The harsh life of a London slum was etched
into her cheeks. Widowed at twenty.
Two sons killed in the battle of the Somme.

Light from the window touched
the mosaic of colour on her face.
A glowing turquoise border gave
a splash of brightness to the dingy wall.

The portrait of Mrs Mounter gradually emerged;
sitting upright in the ladder-back chair
a red scarf tied over her hair.
It seemed to grow from within the canvas
as if it had always been waiting there.

Mary Richardson Brown

Mrs Mounter, (1916-17), Harold Gilman (1876-1919)

MRS MOUNTER

Two cups, two spoons, two saucers,
shoved together, anyhow.
Which of us is chipped, stirs
nothing, an empty cup? How

can I know it's not just you
that's fading away, wearing
out? I am watered down too,
but remember the longing

to see something more than tea
in your black eyes — the promise
of rich, over-brewed love, we
both once drank instead of this.

Clare Dudman

MRS MOUNTER

"Oh yes, dear,
I come here all the time.
Practically a second home."
A little laugh, a little cheer.

"Used to come here with my husband.
In the war you know.
My Archie, passed away not long ago."
A little frown, a little tear.

"Such a lovely man,
So funny and so kind.
Oh, the things he used to say!"
A little laugh, a little cheer.

"My children? Well, they've flown the nest,
Moved away, got families of their own.
I don't hear much from them anymore."
A little frown, a little tear.

Lynne Crook
(Manor High School)

Cherry Trees in Blossom, (1931), Lucien Pissarro (1863-1944)
(detail)

WATCHING A WOMAN PUTTING ON LIPSTICK

Last night the winds of May, the winds of May.
This morning, the ruffled cherry blossom
has thrown its reflection to the pavement
so that it can see itself.

Dannie Abse

CHERRY TREES IN BLOSSOM

All paintings are three-way mirrors.
They are a portrait of the artist,
a reflection of his society
and
they show us what we are.

Pissarro,
who was he?
A sensitive fellow with a delicate use
of the paint brush
and an eye for the beauty of Provence in the Spring,
but
he would always be in the shadow
of his father —
lacking his power, his original vision,
you might say 'self confidence'.

The society he, Lucien, worked in?
Remote, rural,
undisturbed.

And me?
An art critic of sorts
Not a poet or a painter.

Who are you?

Roger Stephenson

TWO JAMAICAN GIRLS

The yellow dress of one suggests the sun
but there's no joy in eyes that look away
and will not face the artist. Is she here
against her will or does she feel or fear
past pain or pain to come? Or did he say
a word that might have hurt this taller one?

Her fellow-model – is she sister? friend?
looks squarely at the painter and at me.
The portrait does not flatter her but states
she'll fight against whatever ill the fates
may conjure up; for certain she'll not be
diminished or defeated; she'll not bend.

They've joined with those immortals who remain
forever young, yet they grow old or die:
Picasso's Child with Dove and Bubbles who
became an Admiral; that boy in blue.
Perhaps when hours of posing had passed by
they giggled, running home, poked tongues at men.

Peggy Poole

TWO JAMAICAN GIRLS

Caught in thought, two Jamaican girls
Unsure of what is expected.
No gold, no pearls, no feminine curls
Only the richness of expression-filled faces.

Dresses seem simply to cover
The frame encasing the being,
Attention not wasted on colours
Since no one around wants to see them.

Examples of ethnic minority
Exposed to strange rituals for whites
Rejected by the unfeeling majority
Our Jamaican Girls' future's not bright.

But what lies beneath their exteriors?
The being encased by their frame
Exposed to the public, their innocent beauty
Is suddenly thrown into fame.

The only way into the being
Is through the eyes that stare back
A bored or a wary expression
Bright whiteness surrounding the black.

Suzanne Pegg
(Range High School)

ENEMY RAID

Flame red backdrop, curling smoke,
Black night tensions, fading hope,
    Water silent, mirroring all.
    Glowing fury, city's fall.

Hatred man-made, conquest's aim,
    Hitler wanted all aflame,
Dockside burning, fear unleashed,
    People dying; evil's feast.

Stands defiant, bomb-free still,
    Liver building, people's will.
We'll outlive him, we'll repair
    All this damage, don't despair!

Black, black shadow, Liver Bird,
    Silent vigil, unperturbed.
    Mersey waters quench the ire,
Beauty shines from hatred's fire.

Antoinette Loftus

The Enemy Raid, (May 3, 1941), George Grainger Smith (1892-1961)

BLITZKRIEG

Like some outrageous sunset seen from Waterloo,
Destruction flowers, filling the sky with flame.
Fires on the Dock Road, two sisters hurrying home
From Blackpool where a brother in the RAF (who never flew)
Was left quite safe; but now, like snapping sparks,
Their fears rise up again and join with others' on the street:
The ripped-out housefront that a soldier home on leave
Suddenly gasps at; unnatural light flooding the parks;
Young girls (excited or afraid) beneath a kitchen table
In a street in Seaforth, all its windows patched with black:

These are the legends we absorbed: they now come back
To children of the Welfare State who are not able
To imagine how a world of wooden huts dispensing orange juice,
Cod liver oil, and ration-books now items in a junk-shop sale
Grew out of this: dark raids, the siren's sudden wail,
A night of restless fear groping towards dawn's truce.
The wardrobe in my parents' room, whose stippled door
Of deep-embedded Blitztime glass was like a tale
Our childish fingers traced in halting Braille,
Was all we had to touch of that imagined War.

Nicholas Murray

HAIKU

Liverpool blazes
vaulted by hell's deadly flames
enemy hate erupts.

Liver birds stand staunch
silent supply ships slip by
watchers count the cost.

Alan Stanbury

Landscape of the Moon's Last Phase, (1943-44), Paul Nash (1889-1946)

LANDSCAPE OF THE MOON'S LAST PHASE
(A Sailor's Warning)

Sinking slowly to the West
A full moon dips towards the month's final lunar period.

Rays of red morning
Blaze over the equinoctial landscape
At Wittenham Clumps, lighting at dawn trees which now grow
On ancient earthworks,
Long abandoned
For verandas
On which the artist here sits
On Boar's Hill
In the bat-flitting cloisters of his mind.

Twice in a lifetime
The sun had both risen and set
On battle-torn landscapes,
Littered with the corpses of our sisters and of our brothers.

No corpses litter this Nash landscape.
It is not peopled with the living
But the trees grow on the stockade site.

The moon held on the hill
Will set,
The sun will rise
Towards another calendar year,
Another summer solstice.

Warriors will stand again
On other hills and plains,
In other forests and jungles,
On other earthworks,
But the earth will continue to work
In her appointed place in the solar system.
There will always be another phase.

John Curry

Landscape of the Moon's Last Phase, (1943-44) Paul Nash, (1889-1946)

YOUTH

Trees mass like sheep,
heads together, conferring.
They are white-fringed like Alps by the backwash
of the light that's beyond them. On this side,
their frustration glows red at us.

I have been here,
with a man and a woman in a brown dress.
A farmer shouted at us.
All our lives were unravelling,
mine, hers, her lover's.

The moon hauls blood
through the world like a long seine.
Like the desired hand at a garden party,
she smooths the long flank of a hill.
Who is where they want to be?

The moon is a wild wind the staunch trees
cannot withstand.
They curl in, defeated, like waves.
They are the moon's slaves.
They shine back at her all night with dumb love.

Lachlan Mackinnon

INTERIOR AT PADDINGTON

I woke in the discomfort of a bath.
Where have I been, what did I do last night?
I drank too much and then I had a fight,
with a plant, I think.

Then Freud got me up
and with persuasion I stood
my head heavy like wood.
I was unclothed and clothed like a doll
and placed in a pose
next to this bloody plant!

What?
Words dropped like stones on my head,
the pain of foreign vocal chords.
I want my bed,
or a cigarette would do.

What's that you say?
A little to the left?
I can't quite care.

There is a crack, a fault line
across my brain.
Memory seeping out all night,
in a million different directions
like the leaves of a foreign plant.

Turning bleary eyes to the street
where I stood as a boy
watching the lamplight retreat
into darkness.

Tom Morgan
(Range High School)

Interior at Paddington, (1951), Lucian Freud (born 1922)

INTERIOR AT PADDINGTON

don't speak to me of dying:
death has been and gone

I wear a coat
the colour of the street

the street is in the room:
the room walks through the street

there is a forest in the room

like smoke I wait to see
rare flowers unclench and bloom

Dave Ward

INTERIOR AT PADDINGTON

Who are you, standing there,
showing no emotion,
pretending you don't care.

Shabby raincoat,
ruffled hair,
cigarette and piercing stare.

Your clothes are so dull
and so is your life.
Alone in Paddington
no lover, no wife.

Another statistic
at the D.H.S.S.
Keep your head above water
in a life that's a mess.

Nadine I'Anson
(Range High School)

Peter getting out of Nick's pool, (1966), David Hockney (born 1937)
First prize in the John Moores Liverpool Exhibition VI, 1967

PETER GETTING OUT OF NICK'S POOL

Chaos of ripples grips his thighs
dissolving knee, calf, foot in pool-blue haze.
Sunlight strikes already reddened shoulders,
slants its angle to his waist,
curves to clutch his buttocks.

His rising is birth of other-Venus;
needs no West Wind or scattered roses.
His spreading arms support, their open gesture
leading to imagined contours –
rounded chest, firm belly, penis.

Snapshot poised, he poses.
Droplets on his arms
trace veins, meander their route.
Spray shaken from his hair
whips crystals, spatters hot ground.

Under the verandah, two chairs wait choosing.
Green canvas invites a sodden imprint;
blue plastic fibres, interwoven,
would lattice his skin.
Squat bush, spiked leaves jade the patio.

The curtained room beckons.
Thick folds promise cool and shadow.
Secrets behind the glass prompt exploration
where no glance can penetrate.

Alison Chisholm

Peter getting out of Nick's pool, (1966), David Hockney (born 1937)

PAINTING SWIMMING POOLS

Ignore the naked boy.
Observe the matt-blue pool,
spaghetti-ribboned cool;
I've no desire to be enmeshed
in this water's grasp.

My pool I'd paint ice-blue,
water waving, gold sparks ricocheting,
straight tile shapes dissolving
to a new geometry.

For you I'd floor a pool
with patterning of peacocks' tails;
eyes would watch, chaperone;
purple, gold and green entwine.
The painting I'd transfer to fabric,
designer duvet, sheets.

At night, my water baby,
you'd be lulled
in watered silk.

Fay Eagle

Sea Cloud, (1981), Bridget Riley (born 1931)

DON'T LOOK, JUMP

Long before
I knew about the sea
or of those creatures
darting in its heart,
I would wade or swim
far out, crashing like a wave
myself through waves,
would circle the dancing buoys
and return, glistening,
to the shore...

Now,
having learned just a little more
about tides and all
the hidden depths,
the vicious ways of fish,
I stand shivering and safe
where the sea is weakest —
one foot scouting for dangers.

Brian Wake

DAY SUCCEEDS TO NIGHT

The moon arose
over the hills.
The stream flickered a thousand fires,
reflected, dancing on its silk-smooth back
gliding, gracefully like the swan
seen today in the somnolent summer haze
of the heavy afternoon.
Lying, like the lizard
I drank the light.
A throat parched.
The sun soaked through.

Nigel O'Brien

SEA CLOUD

A title! 'Sea Cloud'
one syllable fore and aft
a small illusory craft...

I stand on the edge of a sea
or is it the River Nile?...in a blur
of sunblond shallows, mud banks, bays
of ultramarine, yellow dark
as sand and underwater light. Watch
lines of ibis or black cormorants passing.
                    Pupils point — to fossils
on a North Sea shore — open wide
the delta of a circling drought, glint
lower away a coaster's gritty salt
coracles slipping through the river mouth.

I read a notice
on the Gallery wall. These shades
from an Egyptian palette
and patterns 'rhythmic, specific, hard-edged'
were used in tomb paintings
to conjure outside scenes, leave
sensual sweetness to a bereaved dead
sunblue air for lucid slumber.

Suddenly I glimpse a source
of underlying light, surfacing
from a pool of art and thought,
disturbing no valley of mournful kings
but hope, exhumed,
exuberant in the shadows.

So, this is modern... and ancient art.
All groping ways are glorious
that touch upon an underworld —
an eye — with light enclosed.

Gina Riley

PORTRAIT OF SIR JOHN MOORES

Is he entertaining friends?
We don't know.
Is he talking or having a drink?
Maybe, maybe not.
It looks like he is watching TV.
Yes that's what he was doing,
He does it often.

He sits in his cosy chair —
He likes it as it is fairly big.
Next to him he has a wine glass,
Which is on his right side.
He must be right handed.
Next to him on his left lies a round coffee table,
Beyond that is another chair which is empty.

He is old and big,
Sitting with the country outside.
Didn't like being painted,
So it was done very quickly.
He wants to get on with his life,
He doesn't want to go public.

Sian Van Oosten
(Manor High School)

EMIGRATING

Mother o' God have mercy on us!
I wish the Lord had taken me
Before ever I set foot on this
Whirling whirligig dipper.
My stomach's slithering about
With the heave and pitching,
Swirling and rolling.
And all of us herded tighter
Than cattle in the pens on market day,
And smelling as bad.
A heave of folk stinking
Of sweat, salt, sodden woollens,
Bilge, tar, rope, timber.

O to be back home on the good earth
In my own little stone house
Rooted solid on the sod.
Hold me close, Bridget;
Sure you're good to me,
As Ruth was to Naomi.
And we setting off like them
To a land of strangers.
My heart is cast adrift,
My mind a swinging compass,
And no Father Ryan here
To be pilot and navigator.

I'm sick at the thought
Of that great English place.
We'll not know a soul
And nowhere of our own
To lie down at night.
Mary, Mother o' God,
'Tis your own courage I'm needing.

Mary Brett

The Beekeeper's Son, (1991), Andrzej Jackowski (born 1947)
First prize in the John Moores Liverpool 17 Exhibition, 1991

THE BEEKEEPER'S SON

I am a beekeeper's son.
I'm cocooned here;
a grub clawing and curled.
I'm filled with dark sticky substances.
I was formed rotated from red earth,
crafted carefully,
but I look as heavy as clay.
My father's skilled;
he proportioned me.

Adolescent longings of the loin
rise in my mountainous hips.
I could be a 'Rogue Bee',
an African-cross they say.
My voyage is yet to come.
You see me through a honeycomb lattice,
a pink brood-frame, empty suitcase cell.
In chambers you see my future;
I'm a key card, a tarot telling all.

I've grown from cells
made from pure beeswax.
My Polish father's pollen propagated me
in deep pine forests.
So what of the fertilising dust?
Let me tell you how.
Having passed days dipping into dust
with brushes, collecting, mixing, masticating,
he'd tried the colours of many a flower,
then, with poppy and mignonette
the pollen cells were coloured.

Look and you will see
rich molasses, sultana-brown
soft, crisp, buzzing dark flesh.
These colour my landscape now —
the landing board in the lakes
and river, the smudged trees,
fiery forest, waiting.
I'm drawn by arms through
a deep and wet subconscious.

Ceri Courtenay

c *Andrzej Jackowski, 1991*
(Oil on canvas, 168 x 233.5 cm)

INDEX OF POETS